How to Rock Restaurant Management

5 Ingredients to Leading a Successful Team

Katelyn Silva

Copyright © 2017 Katelyn Silva

This publication is licensed for your personal enjoyment only. No part of this publication may be resold, reproduced, distributed, or transmitted in any form or by any means including photocopying, recording, or other electronic or mechanical methods without the prior written permission of the publisher, except in the case of brief quotations embodied in reviews or certain other non-commercial uses permitted by copyright law.

Dedication

I would like to dedicate this book to the managers I have worked with that have helped me to learn and become the manager I am today. There are a small few that truly impacted me, my style, and my life in ways and I wouldn't be the same without them.

A huge place of gratitude is for God. No matter where I've been or where I'm going, I have seen that He always takes care of me, even if it's in hindsight, and I know that He moved in order to put people in my life at certain times or allowed things to happen in such a way for me to be where I am today.

Finally, I would like to dedicate it to my husband, who has been so many things throughout my life and my management career. He offers encouragement and a listening ear when I'm down or frustrated or had a really bad day. He offers advice on how to handle something based on his own experiences and has pointed me in the right direction more times than I can count.

Table of Contents

INTRO 6

GREAT MANAGEMENT EQUALS LEADERSHIP 10

THE TYPES OF MANAGERS 18

The Five Ingredients

APPROACH IS EVERYTHING 30

TAKING AUTHORITY 39

GUEST RELATIONS 49

TRUST IS ESSENTIAL (MANAGERS) 57

TRUST IS ESSENTIAL (THE TEAM) 63

THE MAGIC OF MINDSET 74

Mixing It All Together

HATS 83

TIME MANAGEMENT EQUALS TIME FREEDOM 89

CONCLUSION 96

FROM THE AUTHOR 100

Intro

Today is just like most days for you. You walk into the restaurant, prepared for the dinner shift. As soon as you walk in, you know that it's going to be a rough night. There's tension on the faces of your team and the morning managers, everyone is running around like it's been chaos. Someone meets your eyes and says, "Thank goodness you're here!" As you move toward the back, one of the managers approaches you to 'catch you up' with what's going on. But it feels more like they're dumping all the stresses from the day on your shoulders.

Immediately after, you move into a whirlwind of being pulled in hundreds of directions at once, trying to accomplish everything you need to, and make sure all the guests are happy, and that the team members get their jobs done! By the end of the night, all you can think about is going to bed.

How did you get here in the first place? Is this really all that restaurant management is, from one day to the next? Is it at all possible for things to be smooth, and even fun, on a consistent basis?

When I was eighteen, I made some of those dumb decisions that most people make around that time. Before I knew it, I found myself face to face with a tiny human who would spend the next eighteen years of his own life depending on me. I decided that I would do whatever it took to take care of myself and my baby. So that meant getting a job.

After making countless phone calls to all the local places, hiring or not, and receiving enough 'no's to make me certain I'd never find work, McDonalds gave me a shot. It seemed as good a place as any, at least for a start.

I've always been someone that worked hard and believed in high achievements. Regardless of what it is I'm putting my mind to, I've always thrown myself in 100%. I've lived by the belief that hard work pays off.

I tell you this because that's how it all started for me as I transitioned into mommy-hood and working at McDonalds. I pushed myself to work hard, learn everything I could, and help in different areas of the restaurant when I wasn't busy.

Within six months, I was promoted to manager. I won't lie to you. It was hard. I had a lot of pushback from the team, and I really struggled in the beginning to learn how to be both an effective manager, and a likeable one. I asked tons of questions, was open to feedback, and constantly tried to better myself. But I'll get into all the details of what I learned later.

Since then, I've been a manager for nearly six years in three different companies including being General Manager of a Jimmy John's for one-and-a-half years (shout out to my favorite sandwich place!). I worked for and with numerous managers in that time and I've seen a variety of styles. I've seen first-hand what works and what doesn't.

During those years in those different companies, the reason I continued to move higher up the ladder was because I had a passion and a drive for improving: learning more, and learning from the people around me who I admired, as well as the ones I didn't. I took the good and applied it to myself and tried to avoid the bad behaviors I saw in other people.

But I didn't just learn from the managers around me. I also learned from the team members I was responsible for. I asked different people that I worked with what they thought made a good manager, what they liked, and what they didn't. I did this in order to better understand what makes people want to work with you or run for the hills. I was open to feedback, I asked for it, and I was constantly striving not just to perform in the restaurant and at my job, or do what everybody else thought was good, but to genuinely better myself and my skill set.

I've also spent time studying to become a better manager with books such as *The One Minute Manager* series, the *Go Getter*, *Built to Lead*, *What Management Is*, and more. If you haven't read these or any other management books, I highly recommend doing so. The best way to become a better manager is by asking questions and reading from those more experienced than yourself.

In my time as General Manager, the restaurant I was leading saw 20% growth from when I'd started due to improved quality, service, and team morale, which came from my setting, as well as holding people to, expectations.

In short, I have the experience to offer you advice, whether you're just starting out or you've been a manager for some time and are still struggling with your team and running your shifts.

Throughout my career I've learned five key ingredients for managing a restaurant, and it's these I want to share with you in this book. They are: approach, taking authority, mastering guest relations, cultivating trust, and mindset. I hope by sharing these ingredients, I will help you to become a better manager that successfully cooks up results.

Great Management Equals Leadership

"Management is doing things right. Leadership is doing the right things."

-Peter F. Drucker

Congratulations! You just got a promotion and you're now a manager. Or you just got hired as a manager for a new restaurant. Heck, you might have even been a manager for a while and you are looking for a way to grow yourself and your team.

Whether you've never been a manager before and you have a lot of questions, or you have been a manager for some time, and you have either struggled or you have things you would like to work on, what I'm going to share with you in this book will make you more successful.

What really makes a good manager, anyway? If you're like me, and you've been in the restaurant business for a while, you've probably experienced both what people would consider 'good' and 'bad' managers.

As a team member working in a place with a variety of managers, you probably used to walk in and the first thing you asked was who the manager was for that shift. Why? Because this tells you everything about how your shift will go.

You either had Dave, the manager that kept everything upbeat, flowing smoothly with minimal complaints (which meant minimal food that had to be re-done), and you genuinely left feeling like you were good at something.

Or you had Bill, who seemed to radiate misery to everyone around him and didn't care about you or anyone else for that matter.

Obviously, these are extreme examples: the really great or really terrible. But for a manager, there isn't that much room for in-between. People either love working for you, or they don't.

As a manager, you need to be aware of how much you directly impact both your team and your restaurant. There have been times I've thought, "I'm just one person. How can I really affect *that* much?" Well, let me tell you, you affect *everything*. And if you think I mean just within the walls of your restaurant, you're wrong.

You affect every single person you work with, both while they're working, and in their personal lives, and the simple question is whether your effect is a good one, or a bad one.

Let's be honest. Whether you have a really bad day at work, or a really good day, you are probably going to talk about it. For some people that's hanging out with someone over drinks. Or for others it's dumping the day on your spouse or roommate. Maybe something different for others, like some crazy long post on Facebook. But whatever the case, you're talking about it.

As a manager, you can make it a really great day or a really bad day for your entire team. Then each of them leaves and talks about it with at least someone, if not many other people. Afterward, each member of your team is going to either eagerly want to come in to work the next day, or absolutely dread it. This turns into a cycle, and let's face it, if they're dreading it, they might be stressed out at home, losing sleep, or any other number of ways people deal with their woes.

Are you starting to see how much effect you can have?

Well, if you're reading this book, that hopefully means you're the kind of person who wants to do the best you can and have a positive impact. But how do you have that positive impact instead of a negative one?

First off, if you don't care, neither will your team. Sure, at the most basic, a manager is in charge of a shift, telling everyone when they can leave and what tasks need to be done. But if you've just been going in, running the shift, and leaving – sorry but you're completely missing what you're supposed to be doing. Anyone can do that. And they do. What separates just running a shift from actually being a really great manager is...

Leadership.

Don't get me wrong. Your first priority is to be able to run a great shift. Once you have that under control, most everything else will follow. In fact, most management training teaches you how to do just that.

Learning to run your shift in your restaurant isn't something that I can spell out for you or give you three easy steps to learn. This is something you have to learn from experience. But I can give you tips on how to make the best of the experience and learn as quickly as possible.

For one, ask lots of questions. Ask people around you: your fellow managers, your coworkers, your team, your boss, and ask about anything you might need to know for running a shift. This might be how to make a game plan and follow it. How to make a backup plan for when your plan fails. How to best move yourself around the restaurant to make sure things run smoothly – any tips or advice they can offer.

Chaos happens in restaurants when you're so overwhelmed with business, and so understaffed for it, that all you can manage is to move as quickly as possible to get every order filled. The best tip I can give you in these times is to step away for just long enough to call a fellow manager, or even your boss, and ask whoever it is to call extra help for you. You may only have time for that one call – but in my own experience that's been enough to get the extra hands we needed to take care of the guests.

Times aren't always like this, though, and it's important to learn how to best manage the restaurant during the slow times too. As you receive answers from your fellow managers, be open to feedback. As much as it can be difficult to swallow, it can ultimately only help you. Plus, getting the input of those around you will significantly impact your ability to run your shift on your own.

But if you want to become a great manager, you have to go beyond just running a good shift. Without building your team and leading them, you won't be able to go beyond simply running a shift. A manager is only as good as his team.

Without being a leader, you can't expect to have any followers. Your team is your responsibility to lead, and if you're not doing that, you're failing them. Believe it or not, your team does look up to you. They look to you to help when they are in a bind, give them coaching and direction, handle issues that come up, make decisions, and even get rid of people that are a hindrance to the team's performance.

Yikes! That is a lot of responsibility.

But in order to do all of those things effectively and maintain your team's respect, you have to take responsibility. You must learn to be a leader. If this isn't something you're interested in, stop reading right now. Because the rest of this book is going to be detailing leadership, what it really looks like, and how it is used to impact your restaurant and build your team.

You need to know and understand your power and influence. As they say, everything rolls downhill. To some extent, it's true that you are also impacted further uphill by your bosses. But you need to remember that you still have power and you must learn how to wield it. Even if you're the only person in the whole place that does it right.

Why?

Well, when your bosses start seeing everything you're doing, it makes you stand out. And that means a potential promotion. But there's more to it than that. It creates a feeling of consistency and trust with your team. They know they can depend on you, and then they will follow your lead and deliver results for you.

So how do you become a good leader?

Start with the basics. Practice what you preach, and don't be above doing anything in the restaurant. Your team will know if you make them do something you're not willing to do yourself, and they'll resent you for it.

I know what you're thinking. *"What about delegation?"*

Delegation is critical to successful management, of course. And most of the time, your focus won't be doing the random tasks that usually are delegated, such as cleaning the restrooms. But there will be moments when you will have to do these things simply because the rest of the team is serving the guests, and doing the mundane things in these times will mean a lot to them. It shows you have their back.

As a result, your team will be willing to do the small things you ask – because they know you would do the same for them (not just because you're the boss. That only goes so far).

Now, I don't mean to say that you should let your team walk all over you and do every little thing yourself, either. If you do, they will take full advantage of you – and leave you with no time for the things you actually need to accomplish as a manager. There's a balance to be struck.

But before we get into that sticky mess, let me just say that leadership and good management is not easy. It will be a wakeup call and it will test you and stretch you. Your responsibility is learning how to be effective and to becoming more than you are for yourself and your team.

Becoming a great manager is not easy. But it's something you can do and can accomplish. It's just a matter of time and how much you push yourself to learn.

Food For Thought

- A good manager is a good leader. (Easier said than done, but you can do it!) Part of that means doing the little things that begin to build trust with your team.

- You, as the manager, directly impact your restaurant and your team. What impact are you having, and what impact do you want to have?

- If you're a new manager, you must learn the basics of running your shift, which requires experience. But never fear! You can master this by asking questions and calling for help when needed.

The Types of Managers

"Remember the difference between a boss and a leader: a boss says go, a leader says, 'Let's go!'"

-E.M. Kelly

Before we can truly understand the ingredients of a great leader, we need to talk about what's not, as well as some common mistakes that are made.

I want to briefly talk about where many managers go wrong. If you're reading this and you're a new manager, I'll take a moment and tell you about being a new manager. I'll share with you some common mistakes and some common reactions, both from you as the new manager and from the team you're now responsible for.

One instinct for many managers is letting the new position go to the head. They're thinking, "I'm officially the boss!" and go on a power trip. They try to make everybody do what they think needs to be done or try to demonstrate their new power over them. Especially when they have people that question their position or won't listen to what they have to say.

If you're like me, and you got promoted after a short period of time, or you're brand new to the restaurant you're in, you might be dealing with some backlash from the team. What do I mean by this? I mean the team members that have been there for a really long time, and that know a lot. They start to test you, question you, and even complain that they weren't promoted when you were. We will address in more detail later how to adequately deal with outbursts from the team, but because we're talking about where many go wrong, it's important to recognize what not to do.

Some managers, as I mentioned, attempt to exert power over the others and 'prove' that they're the new boss and therefore what they say goes. This is a very bad move. Inserting yourself and bearing down on the team will only cause bitterness and resentment. The best thing you can do is sit down with each person individually and have a more personal conversation with them.

If it's within your first days of working with a new team, take the time to introduce yourself and reach a more personal level with that team member. Try to get on the same page and get to know them a bit as well. If you're working with a team you used to be a member of, explain that you are the new manager, and that if they have a problem or issue, you'd appreciate if they would give you feedback in a respectful manner, and let you know how you can help them. Let them know you're there to help the team and that you'll have their back. Then, especially if the backlash continues, whether this is a new team or one you're familiar with, calmly tell them not to disrespect you as the manager and if you have to, walk away.

Remember this too: if there are certain members of the team that ask why you and not them, ask them if they've mentioned their interest in management, and encourage them to pursue it if it's something they really want.

Be prepared for a negative reaction. Not everyone will immediately change their tune. If you have to get another manager involved or even documentation, that's okay and you should. But most of the time, people will respect that you're being genuine and want to do a good job.

Simply give it time. You will demonstrate your abilities as you learn and experience how to run a shift and, in time, they will be able to accept you as their manager. More often than not, all you need is an opportunity to help them out and really gain their respect.

I've talked about some of the things you should be aware of if you're a new manager. I firmly believe that knowledge is power, and sometimes just being aware that something is happening is enough to prevent issues. If you're conscious of something, then you can be proactive instead of reacting after a problem's already happened.

If you're not a new manager, you're probably ready for some of those tips I mentioned. This chapter will delve into some of that. I'll share with you my management style and why I believe it's so effective.

Before I share my style, though, I'll ask, what's yours? Of course, everyone likes to imagine they have a great team that really likes them, but let's look at some ways to tell. What are the different managing styles that one can take?

There are many different applications, and many different ways that people will manage their restaurant. But ultimately, there are two overarching managing styles. *Almost* every managing style fits in under one of these two categories and those are:

- The Numbers or Science Manager and
- The People or Human Resources Manager.

For this book, I'm just going to say 'numbers' or 'people'.

We've all worked for at least one, if not multiple versions of, these types of managers. Overall, there are some characteristics that each have which positively and negatively impact their restaurant and team.

The Numbers Manager

Numbers is usually the one that doesn't care much for the individual members of the team. He or she has no interest in your personal life or your struggles. Their main focus is, "Are you going to show up for work?" and "Will you do your job to my satisfaction?" Numbers is usually seen as harsh or even a tyrant. They are very results-oriented and care a lot about the reports and the money.

Another term that I use for the Numbers manager is 'the boss'. The boss tells you what to do. They may or may not demonstrate it, and may not know how to do the tasks themselves. They're unsympathetic, usually. They expect you to do the job and what they ask regardless of your feelings or abilities. They feel that you're replaceable. They're fire-ready, meaning they could fire you at any moment, for anything, regardless of how much you've learned or whether or not you deserve it.

Numbers usually gets results and typically looks great on paper. He or she may or may not have issues with the shift, but the reason is that people are afraid or intimidated. Numbers might try to convince you they care – but ultimately, their actions give them away. They'll do what it takes to get things done without first considering the consequences or the impact it will have on the team and the restaurant. Numbers may or may not even realize he or she is creating frustration and often, due to achieving the desired results, feels as though he or she has a great team and a good reputation. However, things underneath the surface are typically much more chaotic than they appear.

The positive is clear here: this type of manager is usually very good at getting results – at least in the short-term. The team members are too afraid to try and fight back or attempt to get away with doing less than is expected. And because of that, performance is pretty high. However, attitudes and morale aren't usually that great and eventually, these managers will have high turnover problems.

The People Manager

On the flipside, People is the exact opposite. He or she either doesn't care about the results, or if so, it's only enough to get by.

People wants to be everyone's friend and disregards appropriate manager-team relationships. People doesn't often have good boundaries and may even hang out with the team outside of work. (If you're one of these, and you're thinking, *"But... what's wrong with that?"*, let me explain right now). The People manager doesn't have the respect of the team. Period. The team may like that manager as a person, but they will walk all over them and get away with as much as they can. Because they know they can. And the People manager will often let it slide to avoid damaging the 'friendship' he or she thinks is present.

In businesses in general, there are always two types of employees. The 'go-getters' or 'A-players', that give their all every day without being asked, and the 'bodies': the ones who are just there to get a pay-check and have to be prodded to do a good job.

One reason the People manager's approach is bad is because the lack of accountability will cause the A-players to get frustrated. They will begin to feel as though they are the only ones doing the job that is supposed to be getting done, while others get away with doing less, for the same pay! Either your hard-working members will begin slacking also, or they'll simply quit. You will lose your best people and your team and your restaurant will suffer significantly.

While on one token, it's great to have friends at work because having people you enjoy being around will also mean you'll enjoy your work place, there are specific manager-team professional boundaries that must not be crossed under any circumstances.

Whether you're a new manager or a seasoned one, regardless of everything else you do in the restaurant, it's critical that you learn to remain professional. For some, this might seem like I'm stating the obvious. But I've encountered managers who have been managing for five, ten, even fifteen years and struggle with being professional. The term is used a lot, but it's not always specified what it really means. And if you aren't professional, this can really hurt your relations as a manager with your team.

This is even more important for those of you who have just been promoted, and you're used to hanging out with the people you're now in charge of. Those same people have maybe even witnessed you during some embarrassing moments, and respecting and seeing you as someone who will hold them accountable might be difficult. Remaining professional and making distinct boundaries can make it clear to them that that type of relationship with them is off the table and that you're really serious about this new position in your job.

What exactly are these professional boundaries, anyway?

The term professional is often heard when it comes to how managers relate to their team. When someone says "professional", what pops into your mind? Maybe it's the image of a woman with a clipboard, hair in a bun, and dressed in a blouse and pencil skirt. Or perhaps it's a man with a suit and a briefcase. Perhaps you immediately imagine a lawyer, a secretary, or a psychologist. Essentially someone associated with a desk job and lots of paper or computer work. Or both. Perhaps you imagine someone who makes a ton of money or works in the corporate sphere with a nice 8-5 with weekends off.

Let's completely break that image. I'll ask you something. Would you say that being a restaurant manager is a professional field?

In my experience, anyone can be considered a professional *in their field*. It's all really about behavior.

I'll say it again, because this part is important. Professionalism is all about *behavior*.

It's true that a professional should dress well and hold themselves with good posture. But dressing well doesn't necessarily mean you're always in a business suit. Your dress could be in a pair of jeans and a work shirt or even a regular work uniform.

Of course, if someone comes in with a uniform that is crisp and sharp as opposed to dirty and creased, they maintain good hygiene, their hair is clean and done, and they are prepared and ready to take on the day, they will *look* more professional.

But really, a professional, in general, goes beyond the look and should be polite, courteous, and respectful, whether this is in their approach toward the rest of the team, or the guests in the restaurant. This also applies to profanity. A professional is someone that should avoid profanity out of respect for others. They may slip up now and then, but absolutely wouldn't use it in front of the guests.

A professional is also rarely late. I say rarely because, it does happen. No one is perfect. Life gets in the way. But in general, they're either early or on time, and as I mentioned before, ready. If you've worked in any team environment, you know what I mean here. There are always those people that show up as if they just climbed out of bed. And there are the ones that you know you can depend on to bring their A-game.

Finally, professionalism means having clear boundaries and enforcing them. The professional remains modest, and for a manager, he or she doesn't get carried away with one of the members of the team and let the relationship get out of hand. I don't just mean romantically. Even a close friendship with someone on your team can create a wave of problems. I'll give you an example later of how this can get out of hand, but as a rule of thumb, be there for your team without crossing that line.

Sometimes, the romantic side does happen. It's natural. If you're a manager, and you're finding that a relationship is growing between yourself and a team member, never let this enter the workplace, and immediately alert your supervisor to the situation. Let the relationship then bud outside of work. It's a well-established rule that you as a manager can't become romantic with those you're in charge of for a variety of reasons. One of you will have to transfer out or find other work. And most of the time, it will end up being the one under you as the manager. But this doesn't apply to everyone; if you're finding yourself in a relationship with a member of the team, you're one of the exceptions.

As a manager, part of gaining the respect of your team is in behaving professionally. Overall, a professional maintains a proper and respectful distance physically and emotionally in order to uphold boundaries. So yes, professionals are not just the people in business suits in a tall building or an office. You're a professional too, if you act like one.

This also ties back into being a good leader.

Earlier, I talked about the two types of managers: Numbers and People.

There is a third.

The Leader.

A leader is a good balance of both types. Someone balanced between the two knows when to be strict, and when not to. No one can continuously put out good effort when they're constantly being beaten down or told they aren't doing a good job. Or even not being recognized *for* a good job. There are times when confrontation is necessary. But most of the time, it's not, especially once a good team has been built.

A balanced manager is available to the team, not always locked up in their office. He or she is on the floor, helping with orders, making everyone in the restaurant feel important and needed. They have consistent expectations and they hold every member of the team to those expectations equally.

So now what do you think? Which type of manager are you? If you're a boss, you're probably seeing results, but also some bad attitudes and backlash. If you're experiencing discontent or poor morale from your team, you might be managing this way. Even if you don't mean to. If you're a People manager, your team seem to like you, but maybe you aren't getting the results you could be.

I think we've all worked for one of the above mentioned managers at some point. And we can attest to the benefits and frustrations of both. And at times, no matter which type of managing style someone has, they might find themselves behaving as either Numbers or People.

However, if you really want to see more comradery and growth with your team, you need to strive to be more like the team leader. This managing style is what I have used throughout my career to not only give me the results I mentioned, but to create teams that feel they can approach me comfortably about issues they see. Because let's be honest, even the most amazing manager in the world can't always see everything all the time!

I'll admit I've struggled with this. I do care a lot about individuals and I'm very empathetic. I think to myself, *"How would this make me feel?"* Especially when it's been a long night, we're all tired, and there's still more to do. It's exhausting, frustrating even. I feel for my team but I know that the work still needs to be done. Ultimately, the balanced manager knows how to remain positive and maintain good attitudes even in tough times.

How?

Well, let's look at the first ingredient, approach, which we'll discuss in the next chapter.

Food For Thought

- A common mistake is going on a power trip. Instead of trying to prove you're the new person in charge, focus on being genuine and learning what works best with each person of the team.

- New managers, whether new to the position or new to their restaurant, often experience backlash from the team. Handle it calmly, and do your best to respectfully remind the team that you are the manager, and that you're there to help.

- The Numbers manager cares about results as opposed to the team and often has good performance, but low morale and high turnover

- The People manager cares too much about friendships and often sees poor results and little respect

- Often, neither manager is very professional. Professionalism is respect, behavior, and punctuality among other traits

- The balanced manager knows how to maintain respect while still caring for each member of the team, and holds them accountable to performance while achieving results

Ingredient #1

Approach Is Everything

"You must change your approach in order to change your results."

-Jim Rohn

I've addressed a lot for the new manager. But I also mentioned earlier that I have some tips if you've been a manager for a while, and still struggle in your restaurant.

In this chapter, I'm going to tell you how to build a team that rallies behind you and wants to work for you. And one that enjoys working on your shifts.

First, it's critical that as the manager you resist the temptation to 'have favorites'. No one ever likes this. Those who are perceived as the favorites will be resented by the team, and you will be resented for having favorites. Anything you ask the team to do will then be seen in this bitter light and you'll immediately have moved to breaking the team apart. A team with favorites isn't a team anymore because it has been turned into an 'us' vs. 'them' mentality: the manager and the favorites vs. everyone else. This will do nothing but destroy your respect, your team's morale, and ultimately also the restaurant's success, as guests that come in will be able to sense the bad mood.

No thank you.

There are always going to be people that you naturally gravitate towards. The ones who are like-minded. Who get your jokes. Who are easy to get along with. Who you never have to ask to do anything because they do it on their own. It's natural. We're all human.

But beginning to focus yourself on those people in your work environment will only create the perceived favoritism and will put your career on a downward spiral. The others may even go behind your back complaining about you. You absolutely don't want this.

How do you avoid this terrible perception?

By mastering the first ingredient.

Approach

There are three aspects of approach when it comes to the team: task-approach, persona-approach, and in-common-approach.

Task-Approach

As it suggests, the first part of approach is learning how to get what you need – task-completion – from your team. What I've learned is to make the hard stuff about work. In fact, make most tasks about work. Ultimately, your people are there to do a job, and they can do it best when they understand what their job description is and what your expectations are as their manager.

Don't constantly be asking the same people to do the same tasks "as a favor". Your favors will run out. In the words of Dave Long, "Leaders take decisive action." Don't beat around the bush and sugarcoat things, as much as you might think this helps deliver the command. One day, it'll bite you back.

Lesson-Story

This actually happened to me. When I was at Jimmy John's, we had a flood of deliveries but we weren't busy in the shop. I asked one of my in-shop guys to take a couple of the deliveries. And of course, I asked him to do it "as a favor". He said, "No." Well, I had asked, and not made it clear it wasn't actually a question. I was "trying to be polite."

Yeah... No. I was shocked at his prompt refusal and immediately explained it hadn't been a question and I needed him to take the deliveries. Let's just say this was a huge learning experience.

I won't lie to you. I still struggle with this. But your team will respect you more if you approach them confidently. Which brings me to the next aspect.

Persona-Approach

You do need to also consider your approach to a person as an individual. Learning to adapt your approach to the needs of the person you are approaching can have an enormous impact. This is another thing I really struggled with! It's natural to approach others the way you've either:

> a. Experienced being approached or

> b. Imagine you would like to be approached.

Remember: everyone else is not you!

You might be thinking specifically about having to reprimand someone about a part of their job or something else. It does happen. It's not fun. Out of respect for my team, I always pull someone aside if I have an issue instead of 'beating them down' in front of the entire team. I would expect the same courtesy from anyone. Some people prefer for you to just say it regardless of who's around, but I tend to pull them aside anyway as a show of respect.

Obviously, there are times when an outburst will happen. You're in the middle of a shift, everything is crazy, and someone has a break-down, whether that be crying or shouting. There are guests to tend to, orders to hand out. But in these times it is *even more critical* to pull that person aside and make it clear you care while still enforcing boundaries. Ask one of the stronger members of the team to fill in for a moment, and take that person to sit down for a moment.

If it's someone being irate, you may have to calmly ask them to leave and return to work on another shift, or even explain to them their reaction will not be tolerated, but you're there to listen and help if there is an issue they are having, as long as they can communicate it calmly.

If someone is emotionally overwhelmed to the point of tears, they may just need a hug or calm words. You're there for them and will help in any way you can. If the team member can't calm down, you may simply need to send them home and do your best to make sure everything runs smoothly without them. That's part of being a manager! Whether you send them home or they are able to return to their shift, return to the floor as quickly as you can but only after appropriately handling the situation.

These situations happen. However, what I mean by the approach here is coaching. Everyone is different in the way they want to be coached or approached with feedback about their job. Some people like it to be one-on-one and personal. Others like it to be light-hearted and fun and they'll still get the message. Some people want you to get straight to the point while others need to hear good they're doing first before you hit them with the improvements.

Remember, be respectful. Don't call them out in front of everyone or in an embarrassing way. Pull them aside quietly and in a way that makes them realize what they are doing without feeling attacked. Don't be mean or underhanded. Don't be passive aggressive. Be honest. Straightforward. And do what you say you'll do.

Never ever make things about the person, their personality, or things they can't control. It's always about performance and work. Any person can always work better, learn more skills, and achieve greater things. You can't change who someone else is. But you can change how someone behaves. This is crucial when correcting a team member.

As I mentioned earlier, it's important when you approach someone that you pull them aside and behave in a respectful manner. Remember, when you're correcting someone, never make it about who they are or tell them they're a bad person. Never use language such as "you're really dumb, why haven't you gotten his yet?"

Instead, tell them it's about performance. They've had chances to learn and they're not doing it well. And always ask them how you can help. Ask them, "What can I do for you? How can I make it easier? How can I help you get to the next level?" This will help your team work harder, strive for more, and want to perform better for you.

This also applies when you do have to fire someone. If you only make it about performance, they can't question your reasons for firing them. They'll know it's because of lack of performance and they won't be successful with you. Parting ways will be much less of a dramatic event. It may still be traumatic for some people, but it'll at least reduce the stress on your end.

Whatever it is, you need to figure out how to approach them, and do it. It's okay to directly ask too. Not all of us are good at simply 'reading' people. I know for me, I've had to ask a *lot*. Don't be afraid of this. I guarantee that your team will respect you far more for asking and then doing it than for assuming you've figured them out.

In-Common-Approach

The third aspect is that you learn to relate in some way to each person of your team. Approach them as someone you care about and not just a replaceable employee. Find something *in common*. Strike up a conversation. Learn about them as a person. It will make a difference. If you do this with *every person on your team*, instead of just the ones you 'click' with, no one will feel as though you care about others but not them. And it will make approaching them about hard things that much easier as well.

Some ways you can do this are learning about their home life. Their family. Why are they working and what are their specific needs? What are their interests, hobbies? Are they in school? If so, what for? What are their dreams, their aspirations? And to take this a step further, how can you help them achieve them?

While the balanced manager learns to relate to each person in the team, and cares about them, he or she also is not afraid to let go of those who are holding the team back. Rather than sacrificing the benefit of the team and the restaurant by holding on to the people just there for a paycheck, the balanced manager – the leader – decisively realizes the long-term gains, albeit short-term pains, and lets the person go.

It might be difficult at first as the team has to pick up the slack from that person leaving, but they will be grateful they don't have to deal with the pain in the butt person on the team anymore. And they'll probably be happy to get a few more hours as well, since as you'll know in the restaurant business, most of the team gets paid hourly.

Don't forget also that it's critical as the leader, once you get rid of the bad, that you replace it with good. Otherwise you'll be right back where you started. It's better to have a team of A-players working together, than constantly have to replace bodies that don't care and are holding everyone back.

Again, this isn't easy. I know! But you're the kind of person that can do it. You're driven. You're motivated. You're smart. You can make it work!

Ultimately, a balanced manager is one that cares just as much about results as about the team. He or she isn't afraid to make decisions, set expectations and standards (which they then hold team members accountable to), and give feedback about performance. On the same token, that manager cares about each member of the team in a way that cultivates respect and trust. He or she is consistent, in care and accountability.

Which brings us to the next ingredient. Accountability with the team can only be fostered by taking **authority**.

Food For Thought

- Avoid favorites at all costs. It will be the detriment to the team you are trying to build.

- Approach is the first ingredient. It is the way to begin building a team, as well as a group of people who *love* working for you.

- Make task-completion about work. Your team will be more willing, and further, they will respect the fact that you make the job clear.

- Get to know your team on an individual basis, and adapt your approach to their needs and 'approach-language'. The will feel you see them as a person and not just another employee, and will not only feel more valued, but will do more for you as well.

Approach Is Everything

Ingredient #2

Taking Authority

"What we fear of doing most is usually what we most need to do."
                                        -Ralph Waldo Emerson

I've talked about some pretty big, and often difficult, responsibilities in the last three chapters. You may have already received advice on how to be a good manager, how to approach others, and how to have a positive impact, among other things. Or perhaps you are just figuring it all out on your own.

Regardless, part of the reason why not everyone takes some of the steps above to great management is because of something that everyone struggles with and not everyone overcomes. Fear.

In this chapter, we're going to talk about some common doubts and fears, specifically in restaurant management, and how to deal with them. There are whole books about managing fear, and this one chapter isn't going to do the topic justice. But that's why we're sticking with small, specific, actionable points.

The over-arching fear we're going to tackle is the fear of taking authority. Not everyone struggles with this, but there are plenty who do. Often, this fear comes from even deeper fears such as conflict, the thoughts, feelings, and opinions of others, or even fear of handling something incorrectly. We'll address each of them.

Earlier I mentioned a common mistake with new managers: letting their position go to their head. Another common mistake with new managers is the opposite: not being confident enough about their new-found authority. As soon as an issue comes up, a prodding question, or a guest with a problem, the instinct is to immediately go into reactive mode and look for the next manager that can handle the situation.

This can be tricky if you just received that promotion and haven't quite transitioned from being one of the team to now being in charge of the team. If there isn't another manager around, perhaps you find yourself just trying to put the issue off for as long as possible.

Remember, you're a manager now. This means that this is your responsibility. Learning how to effectively and appropriately take authority is the next ingredient.

Confidently Taking Authority

So how exactly do you handle the issues that come up? I'll give you some tips that I've learned that are applicable whether it's a question from the team, a computer crashing, or a guest that is just being completely unreasonable! (We've all had those people.)

I have seen plenty of occasions in which taking authority isn't easy, especially when the task required is tedious or undesirable. One example was a particular team member who proceeded to question why I was making him do a certain task. Let's call him Steve.

Lesson-Story

In order to follow proper procedures, Steve needed to fill out, in essence, a recap of his shift, as each team member had to do, for us to track his progress and performance. I had previously explained why it was important, as well as how it could help him and help the management team in supporting him. However, the actual paperwork did take time and after a long night, I understood the lack of desire to do it.

Steve asked me as I presented the form to him, "Katelyn, why do I have to do this? You are the only one that makes anyone do it."

Wow! Peer pressure can be hard to deal with. And this is a perfect example of an underlying fear behind authority, which is fear of being questioned (and not knowing how to respond) or the fear of insubordination. And I've been in plenty of situations where I was the only one holding someone accountable, and I was resented for it because they could get away with it when I wasn't around. This does happen.

But if a team member leaves because he or she is being held accountable to getting the job done correctly, they probably weren't an A-player, a great team member to have, in the first place.

It would be easy to think, *'I'm the only one? Well... I don't want to be seen as **that** manager. The only one.'* Or to think, *'Oh well... no one will notice.'*

Stop those thoughts right there.

Think about this instead. If I let this one thing slide, Steve will now assume he can get away with not doing other tasks 100% as well. And further, if other team members see that, the other ones that want to get away with things will also try. I now have to work twice as hard to verify that things are being done, and done correctly, AND the team will resent me for doing so. I guarantee their thoughts will be, *'You let one thing slide... why that and not this?'*

And if that's not motivation enough, imagine my bosses come in and do an audit of our paperwork and discover I wasn't taking ownership of the forms. I could lose my job! This is the case for important tasks like this for you too.

Taking authority isn't just about making the team do things, whether it's things they argue about or things they don't. Taking authority is about setting expectations, and consistently holding people to them. It's about letting people know what you stand for. And believe me on this: taking authority will gain you respect. The team will know that you aren't afraid to ask for what's needed, and with time, and consistency, they'll do it because they know it saves time to just do it the first time you ask.

I talked about accountability and approach in the last chapter. This also ties in with taking authority. When you must put your foot down, there are appropriate and inappropriate ways to do it. It's important to still respect your team members no matter what. And this also brings us to another fear beneath taking authority which is the fear of being disliked or not respected.

So what is an appropriate approach?

It goes back to what I said about learning your people. Ask them what approach works best for them, and then do it. And don't forget to use 'please' and 'thank you'. It goes a long way!

There have been times when I've wondered if the team wouldn't do as I ask when taking authority because they didn't respect me. This can cause other questions to come up such as, am I worthy of respect? And am I even a good manager?

The first way to gain respect is to give it. If you treat your team like they are just there to do what you tell them and cover their shift, but never care about them as individuals, you're missing the point and they won't respect you. And further, even if they are A-players, they will resent you when you take authority because they will feel as though you don't care about them.

I've often seen this quoted as a golden rule:

> *"Treat others the way you wish to be treated. Talk to people the way you want to be talked to. Respect is earned, not given."*
>
> -Unknown

How to Rock Restaurant Management

Leading By Example

The next way to gain respect is leading by example. If you're constantly asking them to do all the work while you're sitting back doing nothing, this will lead to the lack of respect I just mentioned.

Consider when authority is actually needed vs. when you're just being overbearing. I talked about your A-players vs your bodies. The 'just there for a check' people. You have team members that you don't have to ask to do anything because they already know what to do and they do it. With these team members, your job isn't so much to take authority, but to merely verify that everything is done correctly and to your standards. Once you've set the expectations with these team members and followed through, you'll rarely have to correct them.

However, there are your team members you constantly have to monitor. These are the ones to whom you'll really have to make it clear that you are the manager and that there is a job to do. In these cases, it's important to know how to hold them accountable without being harsh and causing frustration.

There will be times that you get resistance and arguing. How you handle it will lead to either a positive or a negative outcome.

Remember that story I told about Steve questioning me as to why I made him do the form? I calmly explained that whether I was the only one that did it or not, it was part of the job and that I cared about doing it right, but that I also cared about his progress and how he was doing on the floor.

I received the advice early on in my management career that it's okay to give 'the job' as the reason when you start to get questioned. When you try to bring personal feelings into it, it just makes it more complex. Some team members may even try to play to these feelings in order to 'get out' of doing it.

As I said before, this isn't to say that making it about 'the job' is the only thing you do. It must be done while still caring about the members of your team. My point is that when the team understands clearly what their job is and that you expect them to do it, you'll get much less resistance and a lot more of fully completed tasks.

It has been a struggle for me at times not to become upset or harshly demand that things be done, simply because they have to. But I have also made it a point to work alongside a team member that isn't certain about a task and do it *with* them.

Notice I didn't say *for*.

When it comes to holding people accountable and taking authority, you also have to take ownership of the tasks you're asking to be accomplished and verify that the team member not only does the task, but knows *how* to do the tasks completely.

This is another fear along with taking authority, which is fear of trusting that something will be done right or even the fear of having to ask them to do it again (and their reaction). It's very realistic to wonder, *'Can this person really handle this task and do it well?'*

That's the thing about building a team and its individual members. You can't expect that they all start out knowing what to do and how to do it, especially together.

As a rule of thumb, if I'm not sure a particular team member knows how to complete something, I'll do it with them the first time I ask them to do it. This gives me an opportunity to demonstrate my expectations, but also that I'm not there to just 'boss' them around. I'm there to be their leader. After I'm confident the team member understands how to complete the task 100%, I'll give them opportunities to do so without me and then go back and verify. And of course, I'll always celebrate a job well done!

Never underestimate the power of appreciation when a team member does a good job for you. It will go a long way, and encourage them to continue this behavior! And not only that, but once you have enough team members that know and understand your expectations, they will share these expectations with new arrivals, which in the long run makes your job easier.

It also provides opportunities for you to delegate tasks to those team members that want to take on more responsibility in order to reach management potential themselves, and opens up your time to work on things for yourself.

This ties in with the fear of failure. The question of, '*Can I effectively accomplish all that is demanded of me?*'

My answer to you is: absolutely, you can!

It's true. Running a shift can be incredibly chaotic, and at times it's easy to get caught feeling like you have to do everything yourself. But if you take the time to develop yourself into a leader, develop more leaders underneath you and a co-functioning team, and conquer the fear of taking authority and all that goes with it, you will soon find yourself more successful than you ever thought you could be. And then, yes, you will be able to accomplish all that is asked of you, and more.

If you are interested in a book about tackling fear in general, check out The End of Fear Itself by Steve Bivans.

Food For Thought

- Many doubts and fears as a restaurant manager stem from fear of taking authority. Confidently taking authority, however, is the second ingredient.

- Learning to set expectations and hold people accountable is one of the keys to building a great team and being a great leader. It's best to do so by making 'the job' the why, which avoids conflict and eliminates the fear of rejection.

- Part of taking authority is gaining the team's respect through leading by example, giving respect yourself, and doing tasks alongside them as opposed to simply bossing them around.

- Delegating tasks, while still holding the team to expectations, overcomes the fear of something not being done right, while also freeing up time for other tasks.

Ingredient #3

Guest Relations

"Hospitality is making your guests feel at home, even if you wish they were."

-Anonymous

There is another fear which I didn't tackle in the last chapter, because it is separate and needs addressing on its own: the fear of guest relations.

Whether you're a new manager or a seasoned one, guest relations are a huge part of your job, and can also be a source of anxiety and stress. I will tell you that for the most part, I don't go a shift without at least one guest complaint. Most of the time, this isn't even something I could've done better or controlled. But it's still my job to do something about it.

That's why mastering guest relations is the next ingredient.

Almost everyone knows the formula:

> *Happy and returning guests = more $$ = good things (happy bosses, bonuses, and even happy team members because they often get more money).*

Pretty simple right? Except for one thing. What really makes happy guests? And why are they important?

Well, first of all, I'll be blunt. The guest pays you. Literally. I can't tell you how many times (in different restaurants, mind you), I've had a team member complain about the fact we were busy, and I've responded in this way. The guest pays you.

We are in the business of hospitality. Plain and simple. If you don't like it, you're in the wrong profession.

Now that I've established that, we'll dive into more details.

Your Team Members Are Guests Too

There are two aspects of guest relations. There are the paying guests and then there are the members of your team.

Your team is your key to making your paying guests happy, and thus making you successful.

In the words of Zig Ziglar,

> *"You don't build a business. You build your people and then your people build a business."*

One thing I learned that has stuck with me is that your team members are guests too. A different type of guest. If you aren't making your team members happy, you aren't making your guests happy. Your team are the ones that interact with the guests every single day. They make the guests' food, and they handle the guests' money.

This is why it's so important that you learn how to approach your team, relate to them, get to know them, hold them accountable, and build them up together as a team. And most of all, that you have their backs and show them they can rely on you. When you talk to your team, consider if you would say what you're going to say to one of your guests. If the answer is a huge 'no', you probably shouldn't say it to the team either. Treat your team as guests – and you'll be surprised at how they'll react.

Care for your team and they will care for you. This goes back to treating your team like guests and the well-known formula. When you take care of guests, they come back. When you take care of your team, they will love you and their job. And they'll also come back.

Of course, there are still times when things go wrong. There will always be someone you just can't seem to make happy, no matter what you do, whether that be one of your team members or one of the guests.

We've all had that dreaded moment. That moment of, "Katelyn, there's someone asking to speak to a manager." That feeling of, *'What did we do now?'*

I'll be honest. The first time I ever had a complaint as a manager, I instinctively went into regular ol' team member mode. Find the nearest experienced manager to deal with the problem. I was terrified!

Lesson-Story

The guest had come in to complain and I think if she could've been any angrier, she would've exploded. She'd come storming in like a bull chasing after that red flag in a rodeo, face scrunched and red and her arms bowed out, swinging back and forth with purpose. She slammed her bag down on the counter, quite literally yelling about how her order was screwed up and demanding her money back and the number for corporate. My goodness, I'd never seen someone so angry over *food*!

The other manager with me calmly listened, nodding along, and apologized. She promptly refunded the woman's food and told her to have a good night. I was absolutely mortified. I was certain I would've stuttered over myself if I had been the one to confront her.

Since then, I've certainly learned all the typical steps. Listen to what they have to say, apologize for their experience, try to make it right as best you can. And most of the time, this is all it takes.

But there's more to it than that. I think the real fear comes with escalation and situations getting out of control. I'm no stranger to what can happen when someone has uncontrollable anger, and it is scary, no doubt about it. But you must understand what's important. And that is protecting yourself and your team.

It really is true that most guests are not out to get you or anyone. They just want to be heard and want something to be brought to your attention. Heck, I've even brought things to the attention of a manager at a restaurant when eating

Guest Relations

out, simply to let them know. I didn't want anything out of it. Just to draw their attention to something they'd missed.

For the sake of this chapter, my focus is on the fear of dealing with the guests that *aren't* just trying to help. It's important to know how to handle these times and these guests.

As an example, I had a guest come in one night as part of a group who knew one particular team member that I'll simply call Anne. This guest proceeded to place his own hair in his food, among other things he did, and then accused Anne of being out to get him.

In this example, I made a choice to protect Anne from being harassed. I explained to the guest that Anne was not the type of person he was claiming her to be, and that while I had no problem getting him a different plate of food, I would not allow him to make accusations against my team member. This guest proceeded to tell me I was the worst manager he'd ever met, and that he would never eat there again. Good riddance, I say!

Of course, this doesn't happen all the time, and you should always investigate and do your best to take a complaint seriously and make it right. However, the instances of a situation getting out of control can and do happen.

I said earlier that a leader takes decisive action. This applies to handling guest relations as well. Be confident in your approach and if you can, ask another manager to accompany you until you feel more sure of yourself. First, do your best to calm the guest by listening, apologizing, and trying to make it right.

But in the situation where the guest cannot be calmed, and even begins to threaten you or curse at you, you may need to do more. If a guest comes at you, step back and calmly remind the guest you are there to help and ask them to be seated. If they persist, ask them to leave the building, and if they still won't listen, you may have to ask one of the team members or a fellow manager to call the police. If the guest demands your name and boss's information, you may need to follow your restaurant's policy on this, but do your best to calmly give them some information that will help. This may be just explaining that you can't give out personal details, but that they can go online to your company's website and go to 'customer service'.

Regardless of what happens, remember to keep calm and remain confident. You are the manager, the leader, and ultimately, it's your job to make the decision about the appropriate way to handle the situation. Always do your best to follow your specific restaurant's policy, but also remember that protecting yourself and your team is the first priority.

Ultimately, when you stand up as a leader, you will earn far more respect than simply bending over and letting someone unreasonable walk all over you. And further, you will demonstrate to your team that they can trust you.

Notice throughout my examples that I've said to stay calm and do your best to explain things to the guest. It's also important when handling guest relations that you monitor your approach the same way you would when approaching a team member. Your tone, your attitude, and the way you respond to the guest will more often than not determine how out of control the situation may get. Don't lose your own calm and make the guest more upset or you'll find yourself in a situation you could've avoided.

The most important thing is to do your best to accommodate the guest and make them leave happy, while also still protecting yourself and your team.

Food For Thought

- Mastering guest relations, both your paying guests and your team members, is the third ingredient.

- Treat your team as guests. The formula applies just as much to guests as to them.

- Remain calm, listen, apologize, and try your best to make them happy

- If you can't, remember that it's most important that you protect yourself and your team

- Don't escalate a situation; watch your approach and follow your restaurant's policies

Ingredient #4 (part 1)

Trust is Essential (Managers)

"Without trust, we don't truly collaborate; we merely coordinate or, at best, cooperate. It is trust that transforms a group of people into a team."
                                             -Stephen M.R. Covey

Your team's trust is just as important as their respect. As their leader, they're looking to you to make the right decisions, and if they don't trust you, they won't stand behind you or work for you.

But it's also important that your management team trusts you. No matter which level of the hierarchy you are, you must consider your fellow managers. In my experience, a person is either actively a part of the team, or actively out for themselves. When someone is engaged as a part of the team, they will take ownership for their own part to play and consider how it affects the rest of the team.

Trust amongst the team is the next ingredient. And because trust is so important, I'm going to break it up into two chapters.

The Managers' Trust

When you go in, do you attempt to set your fellow managers up for success? Or is your mentality, *'Every man for himself'*? As a management team, you have a responsibility together for all of the wins and losses of the restaurant, and the team. When one manager has a win, everyone wins. And same goes for losses. You are not the only one affected by the things that happen in the restaurant, even if you're the one that ran the shift.

Try to think of what you can do to help, even if they don't do it for you. Even if the manager doesn't tell you they appreciate it, I guarantee that someone will notice and love you for it. Whether this is making sure all product is fully stocked or ensuring that the sanitizer buckets are fresh, do what you can. It goes a long way.

It's critical that as a team, you and the other managers support each other and act in alignment – even if you are in disagreement. It's okay to disagree with a fellow manager, but never share this with the restaurant's team members. Discuss your disagreements in private with that manager and attempt to come to a compromise. If you feel that manager isn't listening or is actively breaking policy, take it to your boss.

Why is it so important to be aligned?

When a management team is divided, the first indicator is when a particular team member walks in the door and ask straightaway, "Who is working tonight?" Why is this significant? That team member isn't really asking the surface question. What they're asking is, *'How will my shift run tonight? What will I be expected to do or not do, and how much will I get away with? Will I have a positive or a negative experience?'*

Of course, with different managers and different managing styles, there will be differences in shifts, so it's true that this question from team members can come up even with an aligned management team. But usually, when the managers are truly a team, this question won't matter as much.

Lesson-story

I've worked with a manager that was a wildcard and absolutely miserable to work with. Aside from his swings in attitude from one day to the next, he deliberately gossiped and spread rumors with the team about others, including myself. Ultimately there were several team members who lost respect for the managers entirely. They didn't trust him, or other managers, and therefore weren't sure what to believe.

This example is rather extreme, yes, but it's also true and all too commonplace. In fact, for a time, some of the managers didn't even trust each other and boundaries of discussing things with team members were crossed as well.

Dis-alignment within a management team can and does break a restaurant team apart. Even if it's only concerning completion of certain tasks or responsibilities. Remember my story with Steve and his pointing out that I was the only manager who made him fill out his shift recap?

Fortunately, I was able to bring this story up to my team, and they began also holding the team accountable to this task. As a result, there was less frustration with both the managers and the team due to consistency. And performance increased since each team member was able to see where they were excelling, and where they needed to focus their attention.

However, there are many times when this outcome isn't the case. For example, another time I had fellow managers who didn't care about tasks being completed, with the predictable result being the breaking apart I mentioned.

In the story I'll share, rather than one manager being the only one to hold others accountable, this manager was the only one *not* doing so. We'll call this manager Frank, to respect his privacy. There are several tasks that the team has to do before leaving in order to set up the next team for success. In your restaurant, this might be re-stocking, wiping down, and rotating product.

Lesson-story

On Frank's shifts, the team members knew they could get by without doing the tasks 100%. They knew that there was a good chance they wouldn't truly be held accountable, and if they did, it would be sporadic. On other shifts, the team members would be required to do the same tasks, and would be checked to verify completion.

Because of Frank's inconsistency on holding the team to the same standards as other managers, several team members became frustrated. The A-players began to feel resentful that no one else did the tasks, and even worse, they felt underappreciated for doing them. There were even team members that were not A-players who were resentful that they had to do the tasks on some shifts and not on others.

So what happened? Several team members quit. We lost strong workers, simply because as a management team, we did not have true alignment.

Another outcome to that story might have been the other managers no longer holding anyone accountable, just in order to have peace.

Neither scenario is desirable, and having a management team that supports each other through mutual help and compromise will only strengthen the team and the restaurant.

Food For Thought

- A management team works on being publicly aligned which cultivates trust through consistency with the team

- Discuss disagreements with another manager privately in order to find common ground. If you feel a manager refuses to compromise, get your boss involved

- A dis-aligned management team can break the restaurant team apart

Ingredient #4 (part 2)

Trust is Essential (The Team)

"Position and authority will give you followers, but trust will make you a leader."

-Aubrey McGowan

Having your fellow managers' trust is just one piece to the puzzle. Truly getting to where you want to be is about also having the team members' trust. An aligned management team is a cornerstone of having the restaurant team's trust.

Another part of the foundation for the team members to trust you is that they need to know that you have their back. Like the example earlier that I gave about doing some of the mundane tasks or keeping a cool head in times of tension, when the team sees that you can handle any situation, and that you are consistent and true to your word, they in turn will perform well for you. They know that their efforts are worth it.

And also like the example I shared of how a dis-aligned management team breaks the restaurant team apart, so an aligned management team can bring it together.

The Team's Trust

A huge part of having the team's trust is how you react when a team member approaches you, whether it is with feedback, with a situation, or for help. Treat this occurrence like you would if you were a doctor and they were your patient: maintain utmost confidentiality. Especially if it's something you need to pass along. If you share a name or share it in such a way that it's obvious who it points back to, that team member will probably never approach you, or maybe even another manager on your team, again.

Lesson-story

As an example, I once worked with a manager who ran amazing shifts, but could behave very unprofessionally at times. She spoke condescendingly to the team and said things that caused her to lose respect. A few of the team members had separately approached me about it, and I felt it was best to relay their feedback. After all, how can a situation improve if nothing is done to change it?

I approached the manager and simply said, "I've received feedback from several people that while you run great shifts, you can say things that are inappropriate at times and your approach can be disrespectful."

Of course, the first thing the manager wanted to know was *who* had given that feedback. I explained to the manager that who said it wasn't the issue, especially since it had come from multiple sources, and that I wanted her to know so that she could consider it on her shifts. I refused to give any names, whatsoever. By doing this, the team also learned that they could trust me with issues or problems, and that not only would I respect their privacy, but I would do my best to help solve the problem.

This was a great way to build trust and build the team.

Along with this, it's important that your team trusts that when you say you'll do something, you follow through and do it. I will admit that one of my largest flaws as a manager is that I am very easily distracted. In restaurant, there are constantly a million things to do pulling you in hundreds of directions at once. It can all be overwhelming.

I think one thing that restaurant management has really taught me has been prioritization and organization. I've had to really learn how to decide what's the most important task to do first and then tackle each subsequent thing as best I can, and to also get multiple things done at once if possible.

Let's be honest, a restaurant gets crazy. If you can't organize your own mind, how can you organize your restaurant and your team?

What I've learned is that in those moments where you really do feel pulled in too many directions, it's best to prioritize based on urgency. You decide which things are the highest priority and do them first. Slowly work your way down to the lowest priority demands. If you have to, carry around a notebook to write things down so you don't forget each of the things you have to get done before you leave. This could be a little tiny notebook that fits in your shirt or your pant pocket.

In fact, I highly recommend that every manager have a small notebook and pen at all times. Even if you don't carry it around on your person, keep it somewhere you can easily reach it quickly to jot something down. This has been my lifesaver.

As an example of prioritizing, if I have three different team members that need discounts done for some guests, another team member that could really use my help getting refills, and another team member that needs me to go handle a guest complaint, what do you think is the most important?

Clearly, the guest complaint is. But, at the same time, it's probably the most time consuming. What I'll most likely do is go to the computer and knock out all the discounts, since I can do that in less than a minute, grab a pitcher (which is usually right by that same computer), go by the table that needs the refills, and drop off the pitcher at the next station on my way to the guest that has a complaint. In this way, all the tasks are completed quickly and efficiently. In fact, I may even take the pitcher with me to the guest with the complaint as a good-will gesture to start off. Every bit can help.

But in spite of my best intentions to do whatever it is the team needs, there are plenty of times that I say I'll do something, and I honestly forget about it or, if it's a project I'm doing for my boss, is something I have to put off until a later time.

I will say, however, that I make it a principle to *at some point* do everything I've said I will do. I really used to struggle with this much more than I do now. But with time and practice (and a handy-dandy-notebook!), I've gotten much better.

In fact, on a daily basis I will use my notebook to make a small to-do list so that everything that has to be done that day gets done. And anything that needs to be done by a certain date gets a least worked on a little.

It's also important that you don't say you'll do things that you can't do. If someone comes to you, don't just be a 'yes' manager. Take a moment and consider what's already on your plate and what's in your power to actually accomplish, and if you can't, be honest. However, don't simply say 'no'. Offer an alternative solution. It might be asking someone who isn't busy to help, or asking someone more knowledgeable than you the question to get a proper answer.

Another common mistake is seeing so many things that you would like to be done better that you take on too many projects at once. As a result, you get side-tracked easily or overwhelmed and ultimately, nothing really long term is accomplished.

You have to focus on one thing at a time. I know, this sounds difficult. Maybe you're thinking, *"But if I only focus on one thing, it'll take forever to see the real change and results I'm hoping for."* Or maybe you're thinking, *"There's just so much and I want the team to know how much I care and can do!"*

Well, let me share another small story with you, because I have been there!

📖 Lesson-story

Shortly after I began with Chili's Bar and Grill, I was put in charge as the Kitchen Manager. To give you a brief idea, when I took over the team, they were pretty frustrated with how things had been up to that point and were more than ready for change! Attitudes were sour, results were pretty poor, and yeah, there were some things I really wanted to put into place. I wanted to make a difference and be *the manager* for them.

I immediately implemented several of the things I wanted to do, such as using all of the correct utensils on the cook line, writing down all wasted products, and tackling daily cleaning tasks. I excitedly told the team about the tasks, thinking they would jump on board eagerly. But as a result, I stretched myself too thin. Rather than placing a ton of focus on one area and seeing it through until it became an established habit and culture for my team, I put a little focus in a lot of places and essentially nothing got done. The team did some of the projects, some of the time, if I made them, or if they felt like it. I had to take a step back and realize that in my eagerness to do so much, I was actually doing *nothing*.

There are a couple of things I learned from this. 💡

The first thing is what I was mentioning earlier. It's better to focus on one thing at a time. See it through until it is 100% complete, and then move on to the next project. You'll see more long-term results and gain more credibility with the team when you tell them you're going to implement change. They'll believe that change will actually happen.

Trust is Essential (The Team)

The second thing I learned is that you can't make everyone happy. This may sound like one of the oldest quotes in the book, but sometimes it's good to get a reminder. As a manager, I really strive to serve my team the best I can. I want to make each of them love their job and love coming to work.

Is that realistic? No. But I still try.

I'll be honest, I still struggle with getting a little too gung-ho on multiple projects. But I also have some methods that help me to recognize the most important tasks and then get them done in sequence instead of all at once. The main method is writing things down, which I'll continue to recommend! Having my own personal work notebook is truly one of my greatest management tools.

I'll say this. It's great to have new ideas and things you want to add to help the restaurant and the team. But as a new manager, the most important thing is learning your team, learning to become a good manager, and learning how to run a great shift. Then you can tackle side projects once you've been able to master the flow of your restaurant and adequately learn how to budget your time.

Uniting the Team

Finally, a huge... in fact, a HUGE part of maintaining your team, their trust, and their respect, is holding regular meetings with them. This can be as a group, individually, or both. These meetings can be as often as you like or as is convenient for you and the team to get together – even if it's a couple of meetings so that those that miss one can make the other.

I don't just highly recommend these. I personally believe they are critical to your success as a manager and a leader. These meetings are excellent times to really connect and get on the same page as the members of your team. It's a great time to share your goals with them and your expectations as well as letting them buy in to the restaurant's performance and achievements. The more that they feel they are involved, the more they will care.

If you have to break them up into an afternoon one day and a morning the next day, so everyone can make it, do this. These meetings need to be routine and regular. What I mean is they consistently need to be every week, or 2 weeks, etc. Whatever works best for your team and your restaurant.

They should also be centered around something important you can talk about every time. The point of the meeting is to get everyone on the same page. But it's also a chance for the team to feel like they're comrades united for one goal. It's a chance for you to share with them your objectives while also giving the team a chance to give you feedback and ideas. They can tell you what's working, what's not, and what they think would be better.

Also, anything that you, as a team, agree to do needs to be committed to in the meeting. This way, if after the meeting they fail to carry out the promised actions, you can then follow up and let them know they aren't holding up their end of the bargain without as many repercussions. There will be multiple witnesses and they can also hold each other accountable as well.

If you also commit to something during the meeting, you need to hold up your end. The more that you do what you say you'll do, the more your team will also do what you ask of them. Finally, be open to feedback. Ask for it at the meetings. It can only make you better, even if it's hard to hear sometimes.

You can organize your meeting into whatever structure you want, but there should always be a set time for the team to give you feedback. Do not let them try to tell you how to do your job. Make it clear to them that these are suggestions that you will consider. If you won't do it, make sure you give them a reasonable explanation why not. However, if they do give you something they all feel would really work, as their manager, you should do your best to put it into practice.

This is also a great time to get aligned with your team and give them opportunity to share. Ask them for feedback. Anything that they want to say. And then: shut up and listen to them!

It's natural and incredibly human to be defensive and have an excuse or a reason for any criticism that comes up. Shut your mouth, and resist it. Take time to consider the feedback and if it is unfounded, really consider the 'why's so that you can explain to the team, in a way they can agree with, in a follow up (not at the same meeting). If there is something to their feedback, take it in, share it with the management team, and do your best to make something happen.

The meeting is a great place to ask your team what you can do for them. More often than not, there are things that you, as the manager, and as an individual, may not see around you. In fact, no one person sees everything. But as a team, you can see far more. And I firmly believe that knowledge and awareness is one of the greatest keys and powers to success.

Food For Thought

- Trust within the management team and the restaurant team is the fourth ingredient

- Gaining the team's trust is about maintaining confidentiality when relaying feedback, following through on promises, and refusing commitments that can't be filled.

- Use a notebook. It's your life-saving key to success which paves the way for 100% task completion over time and less, "Oh no! I forgot!"

- Have regular meetings, both as a management team, and with the staff. Share goals and encourage feedback as a two-way street. You'll be amazed at how it brings everyone together and how the team reaches new heights.

Ingredient #5

The Magic of Mindset

"Change 'I can't' into 'I can' and pretty soon you will say 'I did'."

-Unknown

I really believe that mindset is one of the most powerful ingredients to success. Whole books have and will continue to be written on attitude and its effects. And that's because it's so powerful and so important. And that's the reason why mindset is the next ingredient.

Specifically in restaurant, how often have you gone in, and there was one sour person or even a terrible guest that completely ruined the rest of your day? Now think about the rest of your team. It didn't just affect *you*. It affected your whole team and your whole restaurant. And guess what that means? It affected your guests for the day as well.

Think of it as a trickle-down effect. The atmosphere starts with you. When you're walking in for your shift, take a deep breath, and consider your attitude as well as your demeanor. Have you had a rough day? That's fine! We're all human. We've all had those days where we just don't care if the world knows it's not been a good one. But as a manager, and more importantly a leader, you're responsible for not just your attitude, but that of all of your team.

Lesson-story

I once worked with a cook who had an extremely negative view on life. He was angry, and it showed. Every day that he came in, it was like a black cloud permeated from him and spread to others around him, making them angry and uncomfortable as well. I decided to do what I could to help. I sat down with him, talked about his attitude and his effect on those around him. But there was no change. I began to realize that he would have to fix this problem for himself.

But I also realized that I didn't have to let him continue to affect my team and eventually, I had to let him go. Did I feel bad? Yeah, of course I did. Those decisions are hard. But as the manager, I had to do what was best for me and my team so that we could do the best job.

I could share many more stories of people who have had a negative impact. I'm sure you could too. Here's a positive one, and how a positive attitude can go such a long way.

I once hired a guy who was full of life. He was positive, enthusiastic, and eager to do whatever was set before him, and do it well. He was the kind of person that everyone loves to be around and everyone naturally gravitates toward. Sure, he was also a little quirky, but I think the best people often are.

Because of his positivity, his go-getter attitude, and his enthusiasm, it shouldn't come as any surprise that he was promoted quickly after I hired him. But not only that. He continued to rise even past where I was. And I will always remember working with him. I don't think I ever saw anyone unhappy when he was around. He had that kind of radiant energy.

Your Attitude First

Take a moment and consider where your attitude is. Does it cause everyone to run like you're the plague? Or does it cause others to smile when you walk in the building? And ask yourself, what can you do to achieve your desired result?

Imagine you walk in to your shift, and the other manager or even the team look at you with relief and excited faces.

According to the majority of people I've asked this question, a good manager is the one that gets in the trenches, pays attention to what's going on, and is able to handle it calmly. On the flip side, a bad manager is seen as the one who hangs out in the office and expects you to figure it out on your own. We've all worked for one of these two, or both, at some point, right?

We're all human. We all have those days. Those days where we're frustrated, we have personal things going on, and our patience feels like the tiniest thing will make us explode.

That's understandable. But regardless of what's going on in your personal life, it is never okay to take it out on your team. You'll lose their respect and trust in you and then you'll have to work twice as hard to get that back.

Instead, do what you have to do to keep it under control. Go to your office and take a deep breath. Go to the freezer where no one can hear you. Take a minute to pray or to regain your focus. Whatever it might be for you, do it to get yourself together. But don't stay too long. As soon as you're calm, face the team. A good manager can keep their cool and maintain a clear head for decision making.

Once you have gotten your own attitude in check, you then have to think outside of yourself and consider your teams' attitudes. As you can see in the examples above, even if you have a great attitude, there are times when there is a team member who is affecting things outside of your direct control. So what can you do? How can you really bring positivity to your team?

Here's what I've learned. A good manager knows how to keep the mood light, keep attitudes great, and keep the shift going even when everything gets crazy. A good manager has a team that even when they're stressed, they don't always show it because they trust that their manager has a cool head and is in control. They know they can trust the manager to do what's important so they can do their job effectively.

On the flip side, a bad manager is the opposite. They show their stress and create even more stress for the team, creating a downward spiral or a domino effect in which the entire shift turns into chaos and at the end of it they're wondering what happened and how they could have done better. This seems to become a pattern. Your team doesn't want to work for you because they feel like every time they come in, the shift is unpredictable and sporadic. They can't depend on you to keep it together and make sure things flow smoothly. They can't trust you to handle issues that come up, and as a result, the morale of the team goes down.

Regardless of the above, remember: Even the greatest people struggle with being a good manager. Just because you have a bad shift or find yourself in the category I just described, that doesn't make you a bad person. This applies to the team as well.

The Link Between Recognition and Your Teams' Attitudes

Consider this.

You have a team member who comes to work every day with an amazing attitude. We'll call him Tom. Tom is always on time and comes prepared. He does extra, even without you asking him to, and busts his butt no matter what. In fact, let's be honest, Tom makes your job and your life a lot easier when he's around.

We've all worked with someone like this. When was the last time that you gave Tom a thank you? Some sort of appreciation for the hard work he does? Are you taking Tom for granted?

Now put yourself in Tom's shoes. Do you feel under-appreciated?

If this is you, and you've never received anything, even a raise, of course you feel under-appreciated! In fact, you might even be considering leaving your current job for one that promises more.

Now imagine your team member like this. Is he or she not probably thinking the exact same thing?

Obviously, A-players like this don't do it for the thank you or the raise. They do it because of pride in their work. But it's also because of an underlying drive that hard work pays off. If nothing ever comes of it, this amazing work ethic will burn out. Especially if Tom is the only team member putting in that much effort and no one else seems to care. Tom will most definitely go somewhere else. Where he feels that people *do* care.

My point in telling you this is to say one thing:

You should never under-estimate the power of recognition and appreciation. Even if someone says they don't want you to, believe me, they appreciate it. No one is going to quit their job because you called to attention that they were doing great at it.

Now, the way that you go about giving them recognition may vary widely. For some, just giving them a gift card with a 'thank you' is enough. For others, they want a nice shiny plaque they can show off to all their friends.

But no matter what you do, do *something*. And something that makes them feel valued and important. Because if they feel that the recognition is half-hearted, it may do more damage than good.

Recognition is also a great way to build your team. You need to take the time whenever you notice one of your team going above and beyond, or really accomplishing a task they struggled with before, to recognize it in front of the entire team. Whether this means a gold star, gathering everyone together to praise them during the shift, or just calling them out for everyone to hear, you need to find a way to recognize them in front of others for their accomplishments. It'll make them feel great, motivate them to continue doing better, and it'll also make the others on the team strive to achieve more in order to receive recognition themselves. It can only build morale and make your team want to work for you.

I heard this phrase in the beginning of my management career: people leave people, not companies. This is one of the truest things I've experienced. Even for myself. I am the type of person that will throw myself into my work with abandon. I dive in headfirst wanting to know every little part of everything. However, if I feel like my efforts aren't worth it and I'm the only one that cares, you bet I am going to get disheartened.

I have actually, in the past, stuck with a job simply because my boss cared just as much as I did. And I have also walked away from roles, in part, because my boss was a jerk and didn't care.

If you want to become a great leader for your team, do your best to avoid having any of your team members feel undervalued. One way you can do this is to consider their pay. Think of each individual member of your team. How hard do they work? How long have they been with you?

For me, I am more than happy to give raises to those who earn it.

Also, keep one more thing in mind when it comes to raises. You want to use them as an incentive, but only as a *reward* for hard work and achievement. Not the other way around. Again, in the words of Dave Long:

> *"Would you say to a fireplace, 'Give me heat, and then I'll give you some wood.'? Of course not!"*

So is the same with giving money *before* getting results. However, when the results happen, it's important to *follow through* and give the rewards promised.

Other ways that you can give your team recognition include giving out prizes to contests, such as consecutive orders produced within a certain time limit or hitting goals with sales. Be creative! There are plenty of ways to get the team involved. The prizes can be gift cards, tickets to something, or maybe a team member can pick something they want (within a certain budget).

For recognition tips, I highly recommend *Built to Lead* by David Long. It's packed with ways to really shine light on your all stars and motivate your other team members to strive for that lime-light too.

Food For Thought

- Mindset is the fifth ingredient

- Attitude and positive thinking have a huge impact on the environment inside your restaurant

- Before you can address everyone else's attitudes, you need to get your own attitude in check

- The best way to build an environment of great, ready-to-work attitudes is by giving recognition for jobs well done

Hats

"I build community. However, I do it wearing a number of hats."

-Cameron Sinclair

So what does it really mean to be a manager? Well, yes, there is higher pay. But it also means there is more responsibility the higher you go. In the words of Uncle Ben, "With great power, comes great responsibility." This applies to so much, including management.

You now have the five ingredients I promised: approach, authority, mastering guest relations, trust, and mindset. And implementing them will most definitely reward you. Before I wrap up, however, I want to share with you over the next couple of chapters another lesson I've learned as well as the huge payoff you'll enjoy for becoming a leader and effectively building your team.

Being a manager really means helping your team to be better. Helping you become a better you. How do you accomplish this? By learning to wear a variety of "hats". And no, I don't mean cowboy or baseball hats. A manager has to learn how to approach different situations in the appropriate way. They have to evaluate the situation, think critically, and act accordingly throughout the day.

So what are all these "hats" that I mentioned? Well, in discussing leadership, I've mentioned being a coach and a friend (though not too friendly). You also need to be an expert and a personal psychologist.

Let's briefly recap being a coach.

A big part of coaching is approach. A good manager can't always approach everyone the exact same way, because no one in this world is exactly the same. Everyone is in a different place, has different experiences, different beliefs, a different personality, etc.

This is something that I had to learn the hard way. And I sometimes still struggle with it, I won't lie. With some people you have to approach them tenderly and with a lot of care. They're sensitive and delicate and uncertain. But with others you have to make jokes, be a little sarcastic, and be lighthearted. They're a little tougher and want to know you can lighten up and have a little fun. Why? So that way they know they can relate to you and they're more likely to listen to what you have to say.

Ultimately, no matter how you approach someone, it's possible to make them feel attacked. A good rule of thumb is to find one thing you can give them recognition for, and make a big deal about it, and then find one thing they can improve on.

The other part of being a coach is teaching. If you want to master it, you can't simply tell someone to "do better" or even do it for them. A coach comes alongside the team, shows them how to do a task, and helps them master the task on their own.

The steps involved are: take time to demonstrate for them, have them demonstrate while you watch, step back and observe from a distance (in a way that they don't feel you watching over their shoulder), and readdress as necessary. Always be available for questions.

Which brings me to being an expert. As a manager, you're the person the entire team is coming to. They look up to you. They follow your lead. They do what you do, not what you say, to use an old, but true, cliché. If you don't know what you're doing, they won't take you seriously. But more importantly, they won't do what you ask of them.

I know. This is a little intimidating. But have confidence! Being an expert doesn't mean that you have all of the answers all of the time. No one has all of the answers. It simply means you are there for guidance and help in any way you possibly can. It means that you can at least hold your own in every area of the restaurant.

So if you're reading this and you can't right now, add this to your list of priorities. Take time on each shift to learn a little more and become a little stronger in your areas of weakness. Whether this means cooking, taking orders, greeting and seating people, washing dishes, or prepping recipes, you should be able to help. These things I just mentioned are what I like to call "mini-hats". They're the different hats you might have to wear at any point in time during your day that you might have to put on and wear comfortably.

Lesson-story

I'll tell you a little story I heard. In one restaurant where I was training, I learned about a general manager that frequently would go to one of his cooks and asked him to tell him the exact recipe for different orders. The cook was baffled and impressed because the manager always knew the recipe and the precise answers to the questions he asked.

One day, the cook was walking by the office and discovered the manager on the computer looking at the recipe before he came and asked him what it was. What is the point of this? He realized that the manager was not just trying to grill him. He was also learning for himself. He was taking the time to know the recipes on his end, so that that way he was prepared in case he needed to coach, correct, or actually make the recipes himself. This is something you can carry into your own shifts.

Finally, I'm going to tie friend and personal psychologist into one. Being a friend does not mean you go and hang out, get drinks, and tell them everything about your personal life. Being a manager means there are professional boundaries that must not be crossed under any circumstances, because the moment the team views you as their friend *above being their manager,* it becomes more difficult for you to do the hard things.

Let's be honest. There are always going to be those people you'll have to have performance discussions with, and even terminate. It's not fun. It never will be. Don't make it harder than it has to be. But being a friend does mean that you make yourself relatable to them. You're sympathetic to their needs and you try to help them as best you can. It means if they come in utterly miserable, you send them home and do your best to get it covered, or make it without them. It means if their child is suffering you let them go be a good parent to their kid. You let them talk to you about what's going on in their lives and let them know that they can trust you not to spread it around and for you to listen and care.

But remember. This doesn't mean that you then spill your guts back. It means you listen, you care, you let them vent and offer your two cents if they want it. And. This is really important. It means you don't let them walk all over you with their issues. If they have a legitimate issue, you help them out. If they're trying to play you, call them out on it and don't take their crap.

Just like with friends outside of work, a real friend will be completely honest with you and hold you accountable. This rule applies to your team at work. Most importantly, it means that you have their back. If you're working in a full service restaurant, you have servers working for you. Your servers serve your guest. Your job as a manager is to serve them. And not just the servers but the rest of the team. This applies to other restaurants as well. Ultimately, a manager is there to help the team. Yes you're there to manage, but you're also there to be a backup and support.

Food For Thought

- There are many 'hats' that a manager has to wear. Some include 'mini-hats' which are the different tasks that you may have to do around the restaurant any given day

- A coach comes alongside the members of the team and gives them recognition for jobs well done and also helps them to improve

- An expert is there to answer questions, provide guidance, and knows, in general, how things should be

- The friend and personal psychologist is there to listen and support the members of the team, though still keeps things professional and maintains boundaries. A good friend will look out for the team members and take care of them in times of need

Time Management Equals Time Freedom

"You reap what you sow."

-Galatians 6:7

Now that we've talked about all the ways in which you can build your team into an awesome unit, let's talk about what that does for you and how you can utilize it to your advantage.

In the beginning of the book, I talked about how learning to run a shift is your first priority, and then I said that being a good manager goes beyond that to becoming a leader. I shared with you the importance of coaching and helping your team so that you can have more time for your other managerial expectations.

Well with this extra time you've found comes learning another critical skill…

Time management.

I am one of those people that actually did have to make an effort to learn how to manage my time. Remember when I told you I'm easily distracted? Let's just say that's the number one way to waste precious time.

If you've seen the movie, *The Little Prince*, there's a particular scene where the mom is showing the daughter how much time she has to prepare for her new school semester. She breaks the days of summer down to hours and even minutes, and then she says, "You can see how much can be accomplished!"

While in the movie, the example is a bit extreme, it brings up a good point. When you manage your time specifically down to what you are doing and *when* you are doing it, you'd be surprised how much you can accomplish.

There are tons of books on time management and productivity and I won't be able to cover all that is in each of them. But I will give you a few points that will help.

First of all, before you can decide what needs to be done, you need to know the expectations of your bosses as well as your team, and even yourself. Write them down. Make a list of all the things you are expected to accomplish as well as the time frame and how often they need to get done.

For example, some things are ongoing and some are one time tasks. Ongoing would be making schedules which are due on a weekly or monthly basis, analyzing reports in order to understand where the restaurant is in relation to its goals such as labor or sales, or writing truck orders. One time tasks could be organizing the shelves or creating a cleaning system that once in place, simply has to be followed.

Remember the story I shared about wanting to get everything done at once and follow through? Once you've mastered your shifts and built your team, it will become much easier to work on your other tasks. You'll learn when the optimal time to do them is, such as slow times of the day, and what to focus on first.

Part of time management isn't just getting things done consistently, but also getting them done 100% and effectively. One thing that I've done is either the night before or the first thing in the morning, I'll take out my notepad and write down the goals I have for each shift and day and then I'll cross them off as I go.

As a restaurant manager, I'll be honest, it's extremely difficult to really work in the extra things sometimes. You're so focused on actually running the restaurant that other things get placed on the backburner. But at the same time, if you learn how to manage your time, you'll see that you can get a little done each day with the extra tasks so that they will get done over time.

And you don't have to do these tasks alone.

It's okay to ask your bosses and your well-built team for help and support on a frequent basis. Let's say you are setting up a new cleaning system for everyone to follow. I guarantee that if you ask your kitchen staff to help you set up this system, they'll not only be able to offer you tips and insight on how to best set it up, but they'll also be more invested in seeing it become successful as it's now important for them too.

This also goes back to learning how to delegate effectively and follow up with your team members to make sure everything is being done according to the standards that you've set in place. It gives your team members the opportunity to contribute and have input as well as feel a part and feel valued.

There's another benefit to doing all this.

Your work/life balance.

How do they correlate?

We all have lives outside work. Whether that means we have families at home or we spend our weekends seeing the world, we all need our personal time. Work and personal life interfering with each other can be incredibly frustrating.

Imagine you're lying in bed. It's your first day you've had off in a while and you're ready to sleep in and enjoy it.

Riiinnggg!

Maybe it's not important.

Riiinnngg!!

You peep your eye open to look at your phone. It's the restaurant. And no doubt there is some unavoidable crisis they need your help with.

With a sigh, you answer the phone, only to be asked if there's any way you can come in to help out because something happened with one of the team members. Of course, as a leader, and a friend, you'll do what you can to help.

We've all heard the 'leave home at home and work at work' phrase. But there are times when they cross. It's inevitable.

This is where time management comes into play.

If you've mastered your time and effectively built your team to support you, it will be much easier for you to get everything done to leave work on time, and also to trust the restaurant will be fine without you. This will do wonders for your stress levels!

The important thing, no matter what you do, is that you make important time for both your work and your home-life even if you have to go in to work on a day off or suddenly have to leave work for a home emergency. These times will happen. But typically, no one will fault you if it's not a regular thing.

For you, a master of time-management, you will know that you accomplished everything you could for that day which allows you to truly focus on both goals and desires. When you're at work, you'll be able to keep your head in the game and be fully devoted, and when you're at home your focus can be completely on your family or whatever you do that you love there. The brief cross-overs won't matter so much.

Here's some advice I got from a hugely successful manager I worked with: "Sometimes, you just have to let things go." Remember that nothing at the restaurant, even an angry boss, is life and death. In addition to time-management, once you master this mentality, I guarantee there will be less stress in your life.

What's most important are your loved ones, and as long as you are doing everything you can while you are in the restaurant, once you leave, you have to remember that you can do more the next time you go in and leave it there.

Being a successful manager isn't about being the one who's at the restaurant the most and working the most. It's about being the manager that has built the most successful team.

Food For Thought

- Once you've successfully built your effective team, you need to learn good time management

- Plan what you'll do and when you'll do it to see best results

- Good time management, especially in combination with your team, will allow you to accomplish what you need to, which leads to proper work/life balance. You will be able to fully focus yourself on your work and your home life separately which also leads to lower stress levels and a happier you.

Conclusion

Wow! We've covered a lot in these few chapters. But I don't think it's more than you can do. Ultimately, the key to being a successful manager, whether in restaurant or elsewhere, is being a good leader. This means a lot of responsibility, yes, but it's more than worth it in the long run.

To reiterate, "With great power comes great responsibility." Don't underestimate your influence as the manager in your restaurant. You have great power with your team, and you must learn how to effectively wield it.

My 5 ingredients to successful restaurant management are:

1. **Consider your approach**. If you want respect, approach them with respect and adapt yourself to what works best for each team member.

2. **Don't be afraid to take authority**. Set expectations and hold the team accountable to them. Come alongside them and do it with them, teach them, coach them, and then step back and let them take the reins.

3. **Cultivate trust** with your fellow managers and your restaurant team. Verify that the tasks are being done according to your expectations, but remember that allowing your team to take part will build them up.

Allow them to give input and participate in the end goals.

4. **Master guest relations.** Treat your team members like guests. Care for them and invest in them. How can you help them to succeed? Handle guest complaints with care and do your best to make them happy while still protecting your team.

5. **Watch your mindset.** And then watch for your teams' attitudes. Never fail to recognize a job well done, and remember the power recognition has in spirits and work ethic.

There are lots of "hats" you'll have to wear: being a coach, a friend, and an expert, as well as the "mini-hats" in different areas of the restaurant. It's important to remember that when you're wearing a particular hat, that you're not too friendly with the team, and you don't cross that professional boundary. The team needs to still see you as their manager even if they see you as someone relatable. That way, when you have to have the hard conversations, it doesn't make it harder than it has to be.

After giving you the above ingredients, it is your job to use them to cook up your successful management career, to wield the combined power of your awesome team and your focused and effective time management to achieve your goals and see balance between your work and personal life.

So here is my plea to you. Don't just put this book on the shelf with the rest of your collection and forget what's inside of it.

Go back through and underline or highlight what stands out to you. And then re-read it when you need a reminder or a little motivation. And seriously, get that notebook. Even if you're not a writer. You'll be amazed at how much of a difference it will make.

Write down the key points you've taken from this or make a print out that you can post, maybe on one of your walls or even in your restaurant's office as a good reminder. Check yourself. Are you following them? If not, consider what you can change.

In conclusion, whether you're a new manager or you've been a manager for a while, these things will help you to run better shifts and improve your overall management performance.

But only if you put to practice the things I shared will you see real progress and change and will you get all of the things I guaranteed at the beginning. In the words of Zig Ziglar...

> *"You don't have to be great to start, but you have to start to be great."*

Thank you so much for reading!

I hope you enjoyed the book and that you see great things in your restaurant and on your shifts.

I would sincerely appreciate your feedback and anything you have to share. How can I make this book, and future books, better?

Will you leave a quick review on Amazon?

Share your thoughts with me, even if it's just a sentence!

From the Author

Restaurant Management isn't easy, as I'm sure you know. There are days when it's amazing, and days when it feels like the biggest source of stress in your life.

I hope that you have found this book helpful and insightful for your future shifts from this day forward.

I would love to hear from you and learn more about what struggles you face or what remaining questions you have.

Feel free to reach out. One of my biggest loves is helping others.

You can reach me at
katelyn.silva@successfulteamleaders.com

Printed in Great Britain
by Amazon